GEORGE WASHINGTON

A Photo-Illustrated Biography
by T.M. Usel

Historical Consultant
Steve Potts
Professor of History

Bridgestone Books
an Imprint of Capstone Press

Facts about George Washington

- George Washington was the first president of the United States.
- He planned the town of Washington, D.C., the Capitol building, and the White House.
- His face is on the quarter and the $1 bill.
- He freed all his slaves in his will.

Bridgestone Books are published by Capstone Press • 818 North Willow Street, Mankato, Minnesota 56001
Copyright © 1996 by Capstone Press • All rights reserved • Printed in the United States of America

Library of Congress Cataloging-in-Publication Data
Usel, T.M.
    George Washington, a photo-illustrated biography/T.M. Usel.
    p. cm.
    Includes bibliographical references (p. 24) and index.
    Summary: Presents the life story of the first president of the United States.
    ISBN 1-56065-340-X
    1. Washington, George, 1732-1799--Juvenile literature. 2. Washington, George, 1732-1799--Pictorial works--Juvenile literature. 3. Presidents--United States--Biography--Juvenile literature. 4. Presidents--United States--Pictorial works--Juvenile literature. [1.Washington, George, 1732-1799. 2. Presidents.] I. Title.
E312.66.U84 1996
973.4'1'092--dc20
[B]
                                    95-46666
                                       CIP
                                       AC

Photo credits
Archive Photos/Ed Carlin: cover
Archive Photos: 4-20

Table of Contents

Words in **boldface** type in the text are defined in the Words to Know section in the back of this book.

The Father of a Nation

George Washington was the first president of the United States. He is known as the Father of his Country.

He is one of the most honored Americans. Washington, D.C., and the state of Washington are named after him. His face seems to be everywhere. It is carved on Mount Rushmore. It is on postage stamps, the quarter coin, and the $1 bill.

He is remembered for his leadership, courage, and honesty. But one of the most famous stories about him probably never happened. There is no proof that he cut down a cherry tree and then admitted to his father that he had done it. But the story illustrates George's honesty.

George Washington was a great military leader. He led soldiers to victory in the Revolutionary War. After the war, he led the citizens of a new nation, the United States of America.

George Washington's face appears on the $1 bill.

The Early Years

George was born in Westmoreland County, in the **colony** of Virginia. He was born on February 11, 1732. Twenty years later, the calendar changed. This moved George's birthday to February 22.

George lived with his family at Ferry Farm. The farm was on the Rappahannock River across from Fredericksburg, Virginia. His father, Augustine, grew tobacco. He was not rich, but he made enough money to provide for the family.

When George was 11, his father died. For the next nine years, George's older brother, Lawrence, was like a father to him. George admired him very much.

George was very sad when Lawrence died. The two had traveled to Barbados in the Caribbean to try to cure Lawrence of **tuberculosis.** But he died in 1752, soon after their return.

George was born in Westmoreland County in Virginia.

First Careers

When he was 16, George became a land **surveyor.** It was not easy work. He had to learn to survive in the wilderness.

George was paid well. By the time he was 20, he owned a lot of land in Virginia.

George became an officer in the British military. He fought in the French and Indian War (1754-1763). This was a war between England and France. The two sides were fighting over control of the Ohio River Valley. Most of the Indians fought on the French side.

By 1758, the French and Indian War had moved north out of the colonies and into Canada. George went to live at Mount Vernon, a house on the Potomac River in northern Virginia. Mount Vernon had been Lawrence's home. George **inherited** it when his brother died.

George fought in the French and Indian War.

Marriage, Family, and Wealth

George married Martha Custis, a wealthy widow, in 1759. George was very fond of Martha's two children, John and Martha. He treated them as his own. In later years, George and Martha raised two of their grandchildren.

George spent part of the year in Williamsburg. It was then the capital of Virginia. He served in the **House of Burgesses**. He learned a lot about running a government.

George also farmed his plantation at Mount Vernon. His slaves planted tobacco, wheat, oats, peaches, and apples. He kept buying land. By 1773, he owned about 45,000 acres (18,000 hectares).

George accepted slavery but did not like the buying and selling of slaves. In his later years, he favored the gradual freeing of the slaves. In his will he ordered that his slaves be freed after Martha's death. And they were.

George and Martha raised Martha's two children. They also raised two of their grandchildren.

The Revolutionary War

After the French and Indian War was over, the British put heavy taxes on goods coming into the colonies. The British government needed the tax money to pay for the war.

In 1773, angry colonists dumped a shipload of British tea into the Boston Harbor. This became known as the Boston Tea Party. The colonists were mad that they were made to pay taxes to a government that did not consult them.

The situation in the colonies kept getting worse until finally, in 1775, shots were fired. The colonists decided to fight for independence from England. It was the beginning of the Revolutionary War.

George was a **delegate** to the Continental Congress. It first met in 1774. Its second meeting led to the formation of an army and the Declaration of Independence.

Angry colonists dumped a shipload of tea into Boston Harbor.

The Continental Army

The Continental Congress set up an army, with George at the head, to fight the British. The Continental Army was made up of regular soldiers and **militia**. Most had no training and no uniforms.

The militia men were farmers, storekeepers, and other workers. They did not like to be away from home. They complained all the time. The regular soldiers called them "long faces."

The Congress let soldiers join the army for only a few months. When their time was up, they would walk away from the battle and go home.

Sometimes a thousand troops would march off at one time. Because of this, George had trouble planning battles.

Sometimes George and his men won battles. But many times the Continental Army lost. They just did not have enough men and guns.

George Washington led the Continental Army during the Revolutionary War.

Valley Forge

By the winter of 1777 and 1778, the British had taken Philadelphia. The Continental Army did not have enough supplies to attack. George moved his troops to Valley Forge. This was a hilltop 20 miles (32 kilometers) away from the city.

They waited there for food and weapons. The weather was bitterly cold. Hundreds of troops had to march barefoot in the snow. They had no boots. Many lost fingers and toes to frostbite.

They ran out of food. Many men got sick and died. George knew that his small army could not win against the powerful British. Benjamin Franklin was secretly sent to France to ask for help. The French sent supplies and troops.

The Continental Army never gave up. Finally, in 1781, British General Cornwallis surrendered to George's troops at Yorktown, Virginia. The war was over. A peace treaty was signed two years later.

George's troops defeated the British at Yorktown.

The First President

George retired from the army in 1783 and went home to Mount Vernon. But within four years he was back in public life.

He led the constitutional convention and helped write the **Constitution**. This plan for democracy was the first of its kind in the world. The Constitution called upon the people to govern themselves. It protected their freedoms.

In 1789, George was elected the first president of the United States. George was 57 when he took the oath of office in New York City. New York was the nation's capital then.

At the end of his first four-year term, George was ready to retire. He wanted to go home to Mount Vernon. The people wanted him to run for president again. He agreed and was re-elected. After his second term, he was asked to run for a third term. George said no.

George took the oath of office in New York City.

A Great Leader

As president, George organized the government and made many important decisions. He was very careful in everything he did. George knew he was setting the structure for future presidents. Though he never lived there, he planned the White House and the capital city of Washington, D.C.

In his farewell address, George told Americans not to go to war with other countries. Then he returned to Mount Vernon. He was 65.

One cold, rainy day, George went for his usual horse ride around Mount Vernon. The next morning he had a sore throat.

A doctor drained blood from George to make him feel better. It was a common way to treat many illnesses then. But George got weaker. He died on December 14, 1799. The United States of America had lost its first great leader.

In his farewell address, George told Americans not to go to war with other countries.

Words from George Washington

"Observe good faith and justice towards all nations. Cultivate peace and harmony with all."

From Washington's farewell address,
September 19, 1796.

"Rise early, that by habit it may become familiar, agreeable, healthy and profitable. It may, for awhile, be irksome to do this, but that will wear off; and the practice will produce a rich harvest forever thereafter, whether in public or private walks of life."

From Washington's letter to George Washington Parke Custis, Martha's grandson whom they raised as a son, 1797.

Important Dates in George Washington's Life

1732 – Born in Westmoreland County, Virginia

1754 – Begins serving in the army in the French and Indian War

1758 – Elected to Virginia House of Burgesses

1759 – Marries Martha Dandridge Custis

1775 – Revolutionary War begins, becomes commander-in-chief

1776 – Declaration of Independence

1777 – Winter at Valley Forge

1781 – Defeats General Cornwallis at Yorktown

1787 – Presides over Constitutional Convention

1789 – Elected first president of the United States

1792 – Re-elected as president

1797 – Leaves office after refusing a third term

1799 – Dies at Mount Vernon

Words to Know

colony—group of people who settle in a distant land but remain under control of their native country. The 13 British colonies in North America became the original United States.

Constitution—the document that is the basic law of the United States

House of Burgesses—the lower house of the colonial legislature of Virginia

inherit—receive from someone who has died

militia—citizens who are not professional soldiers called to serve in the armed services during emergencies

surveyor—a person who makes measurements of land

tuberculosis—contagious disease that mainly affects the lungs

Read More

Adler, David A. *George Washington: Father of Our Country.* New York: Holiday House, 1988.

Giblin, James Cross. *George Washington: A Picture Book Biography.* New York: Scholastic, 1992.

Greene, Carol. *George Washington: First President of the United States.* Chicago: Children's Press, 1991.

Williams, Brian. *George Washington.* New York: Marshall Cavendish, 1988.

Useful Addresses

Mount Vernon Ladies' Association
Mount Vernon, VA 22121

Sons of the American Revolution
1000 South Fourth Street
Louisville, KY 40203

Society of the Descendants of Washington's Army at Valley Forge
P.O. Box 573
Valley Forge, PA 19482

Washington National Monument Association
740 Jackson Place NW
Washington, DC 20503

Index